HABITATS
Wetlands

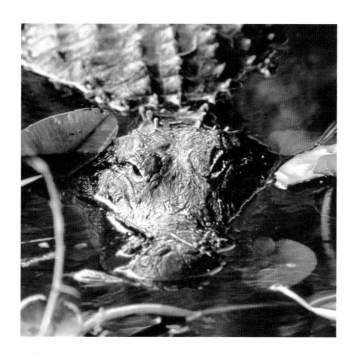

Robert Snedden

A+
Smart Apple Media

Published by Smart Apple Media
2140 Howard Drive West, North Mankato, Minnesota 56003

Designed by Helen James

Photographs by Corbis (AFP, Theo Allofs, Adrian Arbib, Anthony Bannister; Gallo
Images, Gary W. Carter, Bryn Colton/Assignments Photographers, Pam Gardner; Frank
Lane Picture Agency, Raymond Gehman, Robert Holmes, Eric and David Hosking,
Peter Hulme; Ecoscene, Peter Johnson, Layne Kennedy, Wayne Lawler; Ecoscene,
George McCarthy, Joe McDonald, David Muench, Greg Probst, Joel W. Rogers, Paul A.
Souders, Tim Thompson, Jeff Vanuga, Nik Wheeler, David Zimmerman)

Printed in the USA

Library of Congress Cataloging-in-Publication Data

Snedden, Robert.
Wetlands / by Robert Snedden.
p. cm. — (Habitats)
Contents: The borderland — How wetlands form — Wetland plants — Marshes —
Mangrove swamps — Swamps — Bogs — The pantanal — Down to the delta —
Wetlands of Alaska — Wetlands and waterfowl — What wetlands do — Wetlands
under threat.
ISBN 1-58340-387-6
1. Wetlands—Juvenile literature. 2. Wetland ecology—Juvenile literature.
[1. Wetlands. 2. Wetland ecology. 3. Ecology.] I. Title.

QH87.3.S64 2004
577.68–dc21   2003045681

First Edition

9 8 7 6 5 4 3 2 1

Contents

The Borderland

The place where a living thing makes its home is called its **habitat**. A habitat can be as small as a damp place under a rotting log, or as big as the ocean. The biggest habitats, such as deserts, forests, and mountains, are called **biomes**.

Wetlands are unusual habitats. They are the places where a water habitat changes into a dry land habitat. A wetland is a borderland, neither fully a water habitat nor fully a dry habitat. Places where one habitat blends into another are called ecotones. Ecotones contain plants and animals normally found in each of the bordering habitats, as well as species found only within the transitional (middle) zone.

Worldwide wet

To try to define a "typical" wetland **climate** is nearly impossible because wetlands are found in almost all of the

world's climate zones. There are wetlands everywhere, from the frozen **tundra** to the warm, salty shores of the tropical seas. A wetland is a place that is saturated with water for at least some of the time. It may be flooded every day when the tide comes in, or flooded for only part of the year, when the rainy season comes or snow melts in the spring. A wetland may even be permanently covered by water; however, the water must be shallow enough to allow plants to grow above its surface.

Wetlands can be found along the banks of rivers, by the shores of lakes and oceans, and in low-lying areas where rain or meltwater

*Salt marshes are vital
habitats for water birds.*

*The wet conditions in swamps
and marshes make them ideal
homes for amphibians like
this frog.*

collects. A **marsh** by a river is a wetland, and so too are the moss-covered **bogs** of the northern forest. The water that sustains a wetland can be fed to it by tides, rainfall, river floods, or underground springs.

Types of wetlands

There are many different kinds of wetlands. This fact is reflected in the many different names people have for wetland areas, including swamps, marshes, bogs, fens, mires, bottomlands, and muskegs.

How Wetlands Form

It takes water to make a wetland. That seems obvious enough, but where the water comes from might not be so obvious. A wetland is defined as an area where the land is flooded for at least part of the growing season. This means that a wetland can look quite dry at times. Some wetlands are even surrounded by desert! The important thing is that there is a regular supply of water.

The soils in a wetland environment are different from those found elsewhere. Because there is usually a flow of water through the wetland, materials are always being brought to the wetland from outside its borders. This material can take the form of **minerals** dissolved from rocks nearby, or decaying plant and animal matter. The addition of this new material increases the depth of the soil in the wetland.

As new materials are brought to the wetland, the surface of the soil rises above the **water table**. This means that the land becomes flooded less and less often. Eventually, the wetland may disappear altogether, replaced by grassland or forest.

Coastal wetlands

As the name suggests, coastal wetlands form near seashores and are kept wet by the effects of the **tide**. Tidal freshwater marshes

Flooding of the Columbia River across its wide valley has produced spectacular wetland areas.

Marshes are temporarily or permanently covered with water and are home to grasslike vegetation.

develop inland near a river's mouth (outlet). The tides have some effect on these marshes, but most of their water comes from the river and rainfall. Tidal saltwater marshes are found on sheltered coasts, where they are protected from waves. A saltwater marsh may stretch back several miles from the shore.

Inland wetlands

Freshwater marshes are covered with a shallow layer of water and are found around lakes, ponds, and slow-moving streams and rivers. Deep-water swamps are forested wetlands. They often form around the edges of lakes and are wet for most, if not all, of the growing season.

THE WATER TABLE

Not all rainwater flows into rivers and streams or **evaporates** into the air. Some of it soaks down into the ground as groundwater—water that passes through the small spaces between rocks. Groundwater can form huge **reservoirs** of water beneath the ground. The top of this saturated ground is called the water table. In a wetland, the water table is right at the surface of the soil.

Wetland Plants

Plants are very important to a wetland area. Their roots bind the soil together, preventing it from being washed away. Some types of plants, such as sedges (grasslike plants), are found in nearly all of the world's wetland areas.

Wetland plants are called hydrophytes, a name that simply means "water lovers." These plants may be **adapted** to life fully submerged in water or with their stems or leaves standing above the surface. Plants that live totally underwater include wild celery and water chestnuts.

Breathing tubes

Plants need oxygen to survive. They use oxygen to release energy from their food. The problem that wetland plants have is that there is very little oxygen in waterlogged soil. One way many plants have adapted to this condition is by developing hollow tubes that run down through their stems. These tubes

Spartina grass is able to deal with the salty water in its salt marsh habitat.

Water chestnut grows so well in some wetland areas that it is considered a pest that needs to be controlled.

carry oxygen from the air down to the plants' roots.

Salty Spartina

Plants that live in saltwater marshes not only have the wet conditions to deal with, but they also have to find a way to deal with the salt, which is harmful to most plants. A common saltwater grass called Spartina is adapted to life in a salty environment. It gets rid of salt by taking the salty water up through its roots and then producing salt crystals through pores in its leaves.

HIBERNATING TREES

Most trees lose their leaves when water becomes scarce. The trees that grow in the floodlands along the Amazon River, however, do just the opposite. When the river rises up and floods, the trees drop their leaves and grow back only when the water level goes down again. The reason for this is that the waterlogged soil lacks oxygen, and so the tree "goes to sleep" until conditions improve.

Marshes

Marshes are wetlands that are submerged by water most, if not all, of the time. They are rich habitats with a wide variety of plant and animal life.

Saltwater marshes

There are many different kinds of marshes. Saltwater marshes, or tidal marshes, can be found along gently sloping, sheltered coastlines throughout the world to the north and south of the tropics. (Tropical saltwater marshes are called mangrove swamps.) Saltwater marshes tend to form where the action of the tides is not too strong. They are flooded at least once a month by the high tide, and seen from above, they look like a patchwork of low-growing vegetation with a network of tidal creeks flowing through them.

The most common saltwater marsh plants are grasses and rushes. Marsh grasses are tough

plants, and there aren't many animals that eat them. The grasses grow lush and green throughout the spring and summer. In the fall and winter, they die and begin to decay. This is when they become a food source for the marsh animals. Microscopic life-forms (microbes) such as fungi and bacteria begin to break the plants down. The decaying, or decomposing, plant matter sinks into the marsh, where it is consumed by fish, shrimp, and crabs. The microbes will consume the droppings of these animals as well as the decaying plant remains. Eventually, all this decomposition results in a fine fertilizer that

Foraging fiddler crabs find plenty to eat in the mud of a salt marsh.

feeds the following year's crop of marsh grass. The large numbers of fish and other animals living in the shallow waters of the swamp attract flocks of birds, such as egrets, that come to feast on them.

Prairie potholes provide grazing cattle with a source of water.

Freshwater marshes

Freshwater marshes form in low-lying areas around lakes, rivers, and streams. The water in these marshes may be anywhere from one inch (2.5 cm) to three feet (1 m) deep. Flooding can be very seasonal, leaving some freshwater marshes to dry out altogether for part of the year. Freshwater marshes are some of the richest and most productive habitats on Earth. The reason for this is the soil. It is packed full of **nutrients** and minerals so plants grow very well here. Diverse plant communities, including reeds, rushes, and lilies, attract a wide range of wildlife, such as small mammals and waterfowl, which come to freshwater marshes in huge numbers.

PRAIRIE POTHOLES

Prairie potholes are marsh-like ponds that have formed in shallow basins left behind as the **glaciers** retreated from North America at the end of the last ice age. Because they are at a lower level than the surrounding land, water tends to run into the potholes, keeping them wet. However, if there is little rainfall, the potholes can dry up, often for years. It has been estimated that between 50 and 75 percent of North America's waterfowl are hatched in prairie potholes.

Mangrove Swamps

Strips of swampland can be found along the coastlines of the tropics. Where the waves are not too strong to prevent large plants from taking root, these coastal wetlands become covered by **stands** of mangrove trees. The trees may grow so thickly that they form a nearly impenetrable maze of woody stems and roots.

There are about 70 different types of mangrove trees found around the world. They are well adapted to life in salty conditions. Mangrove trees can prevent too much salt from entering through their roots. They can also lose salt through their leaves and can even shed leaves altogether to rid themselves of excess salt.

Aerial roots

Mangrove trees are unusual. Each tree has roots that grow out from high up on the trunk and plunge down into the mud. These "stilt roots" give the tree added support and help keep it upright when the action of the waves is strong. One of the problems for wetland plants is the lack of oxygen in the

The bright-red scarlet ibis contrasts with the green grass of its habitat.

soil for their roots. Mangrove trees adapt to the oxygen-poor conditions by growing stick-like structures that poke up from the mud around them. These structures have little openings in them that can take in oxygen and deliver it to the roots.

Mangrove swamps are home to a wide range of animals. Bird life in the swamps is particularly rich and colorful, including the scarlet ibis and the fish-eating darter. The saltwater crocodile, the biggest crocodile in the world, is found in the mangrove swamps of Southeast Asia and Australia. A supply of nutrients is continually being brought to the swamp by freshwater streams, and the mud carries huge populations of bacteria, algae, and other microbes. The smaller animals of the swamp, which are eaten by the bigger animals, rely on these microscopic organisms for food.

Mangroves are well adapted to swamp life, having developed special roots for support and breathing.

SEED SPEARS

Mangrove seeds often begin to **germinate** while they are still on the parent tree. They grow a thick, spear-like projection. When the seed eventually falls from the tree, this spear becomes embedded in the mud, anchoring the seed while it grows roots.

Swamps

Swamps are wetlands in which the main kinds of plants are trees and shrubs. Maples, swamp cypresses, water tupelos, and some types of oaks are typical swampland trees. The soil in a swamp is nearly always wet and will be completely flooded by several feet of slow-moving water for at least part of the year.

The soil is rich in nutrients that provide excellent growing conditions for trees that are able to tolerate the wet conditions. Some of the most well-known swamplands are found in Florida. There the land is low-lying and often flooded. Forested swamps are often completely flooded by water that spills over from rivers and streams. Even in very dry years, swamps will still be wet. This makes them vital habitats for animals that depend on wetlands for their survival, such as ducks and otters.

Swamp trees

Swampland trees are often very tall and stately. Many have **buttresses** at the base of their trunks. These fanned-out growths help give the trees extra support in the wet ground. Around the bases of the trees, things that look like rotted tree stumps poke out of the ground and project a few feet above the surface of the water. These projections are called knee roots. Several types of swampland trees have knee roots. Their job is to provide oxygen for the roots that are permanently beneath the water surface.

The spreading buttresses of these cypress trees make them more stable in the wet soil.

*Alligators are the top **predators** in many swamps.*

DOWN TO THE BOTTOMLAND

Bottomland hardwood forests are swamps that form in the flood plains of rivers in the southern United States. Native trees include gum trees, oaks, and cypresses, all of which have adapted to life in very wet conditions.

Swamp trees produce seeds that germinate and grow only in dry conditions. This means that new trees can grow only if the swamp dries out briefly. If the swamp never dries, new trees cannot grow, and the swamp will eventually become a lake. The swamp has to dry only once every 100 years or so for new trees to become established.

A rich variety

The rich soils of the swamplands, like those of the freshwater marshes, make them extraordinarily productive. Frogs abound in the wet conditions, as do snails, freshwater shrimp, and other damp-loving creatures. Many types of birds live there, taking advantage of the abundant seeds, fruits, and insects. The tangles of trees and shrubs also provide a number of sheltered nesting sites. In some parts of the world, swamps are home to crocodiles and alligators. These meat-eaters hunt animals such as deer that come to the swamp to feed.

Bogs

Bogs do not get their water from streams, rivers, or groundwater. Only rainfall keeps a bog wet. This means that nutrients do not flow into a bog the way they flow into other wetlands. Unlike river water, for example, rainwater carries very little in the way of nutrients. In addition, rainwater may wash away what few nutrients there are in the soil. As a result, bog soil is very poor.

Bog plants

Few plants, with the exception of mosses, can grow in the bog's poor conditions. Bog mosses act like sponges, holding onto water and keeping the bog moist. The mosses themselves become the major source of nutrients for the bog soil. As the moss plants grow upward, their lower leaves decay and are slowly broken down by bacteria, releasing nutrients back into the soil.

Muskegs

Many bogs exist in the northern (boreal) forest. There, where the temperatures are cool and the rainfall amounts are high, conditions are ideal for mosses to grow. Low-lying bogs, called muskegs, are common throughout the boreal forest. Mosses form a thick, spongy mat on the surface of the bog. Grasses and shrubs grow on top of the mossy mat, and spruce and

Insect-eating plants, such as this pitcher plant, are common in wetlands with poor soils.

▲ *If the vegetation of a bog is damaged, the peat is soon washed away, leaving behind deep gullies.*

larch trees grow around the slightly drier edges of the bog.

Insect-eaters

Because bog soil is not rich in nutrients, some plants have adapted to get their nutrients from other sources. One of the most common types of plants growing in the bogs of the northern forest are those that eat insects, including pitcher plants and sundews. Pitcher plants have hollow stalks into which insects fall and become trapped. Sundews have sticky threads growing on their leaves in which insects become entangled. Once an insect-eating plant has caught its **prey**, it produces juices that slowly digest it, releasing nutrients in the process that the plant can use.

Peatbogs

In the cold, damp conditions of a bog, plants decay very slowly. Plant remains in the process of decomposing form a layer of **peat**, a dark-brown fibrous substance. The peat grows by a tiny fraction of an inch each year, but in some ancient bogs, the layer of peat can be several feet thick. Peat is easily eroded, and if the bog vegetation is damaged, great gullies (channels) can form as the peat is washed away.

The Pantanal

The Pantanal of South America is the world's largest wetland area. It is bigger than the entire country of Greece, extending through eastern Bolivia, Paraguay, and central Brazil. Every year the floodwaters of the Paraguay River rise many feet and spill out over the Pantanal. The Portuguese word *Pantanal* means "swamp."

The animals of the Pantanal are among the most spectacular in the world. To survive there, animals must be able to fly or swim strongly. Hundreds of varieties of colorful birds, such as toucans and the rare hyacinth macaw, fly through the trees, while the waters are patrolled by long-legged ibises, storks, and spoonbills. There are thousands of different insects, many found nowhere else on Earth. The endangered jaguar prowls the Pantanal, and giant river otters hunt the rich shoals of wetland fish. Large snakes, such as the boa constrictor and the anaconda, slide silently through the water. In the winter, the resident population of wildlife swells with huge flocks of waterfowl **migrating** from North America.

Pantanal seasons

The rainy season in the Pantanal lasts from October to March. Heavy rainfall at this time fills up the slow-moving Paraguay River and its tributaries (small streams).

The hyacinth macaw, found in the Pantanal, is one of the world's most colorful, and endangered, birds.

The surrounding land is covered with water. By contrast, during the dry season, large, low-lying areas of the Pantanal may be almost without water. The wetland landscape is transformed into a grassland by the intense heat of the sun. If there is no rain, the greenest areas will be those around the many lakes and ponds that dot the land. Changing circumstances mean that the plants of the Pantanal have to be able to adapt to both wet and dry conditions.

The river otter is a wetland animal with an uncertain future.

THE GIANT RIVER OTTER

The giant river otter is the largest of the otters and is found only in the rainforests and rivers of South America. Adults may measure nearly six feet (1.8 m) from nose to tail. They have big, webbed feet and powerful tails to propel them through the water. Slow-moving rivers, swamps, and marshes are their favorite places. The giant river otter is one of the world's most endangered animals. There may be as few as 1,000 left.

Down to the Delta

As a river flows along its course, the moving water picks up particles of rock and soil, called **sediment**. As it approaches the sea or lake into which it flows, the river slows down and drops the sediment, forming a **delta**. Deltas are usually triangle-shaped, though they can be different shapes, too, according to how much sediment is deposited and how it is worn away by tides, wind, and waves. River deltas are some of the world's richest wetland habitats.

The Okavango Delta

One of the world's largest wetland areas is in the middle of a desert! The Okavango River, in Africa, has been described as "the river that never finds the sea." The river begins in the highlands of Angola and flows to the Kalahari Desert, in the northeastern corner of Botswana. There, hundreds of miles from the ocean, it splits into a maze of channels covering an area of more than 6,000 square miles (15,600 sq km). If the rainy season is particularly wet, the river delta can spread out over 8,500 square miles (22,100 sq km) of the desert. Nowhere is the water very deep. Only a few inches cover most of the area. The Okavango landscape is constantly changing as islands appear and disappear with the rising and falling water levels.

The Okavango Delta is one of the world's largest wetland areas.

▲ *The hippopotamus is one of the most eye-catching animals in the delta.*

Okavango wildlife

It has been estimated that there are more than 35 million fish in the Okavango. Some fish are eaten by bigger fish, and the bigger fish are eaten by crocodiles. Hippopotamuses bulldoze their way through the wetland vegetation, flattening reeds and grasses as they make their way to the water. Antelopes make use of the hippo pathways as they cross the swamps.

Papyrus reeds are the main type of plant along the Okavango. Trees grow on the edges of the swamps, and beyond the trees lies savanna grassland. The changing nature of the delta landscape means that there is a

huge variety of wildlife, all adapted to the different conditions. Elephants and giraffes graze on the forest trees and shrubs. Wildebeest and other antelopes feed on the grasslands where lions and wild dogs hunt.

The Wetlands of Alaska

Nearly half of the state of Alaska is wetland. All types of wetlands, including, ponds, freshwater and saltwater marshes, and river flood plains, are found across the Alaskan landscape. There are more wetlands in Alaska than in the rest of the United States put together.

The Copper River Delta

Alaska's Copper River Delta is the largest wetland area on the Pacific coast of North America. The Copper River begins as a small stream flowing from a glacier and cuts its way across nearly 300 miles (480 km) of Alaskan landscape to the Pacific Ocean. It quickly grows in size and power as a

 The Copper River Delta is a vast, beautiful wetland area.

number of other rivers feed into it. Eventually it reaches the Gulf of Alaska, where it spreads out into a 60-mile-wide (100 km) delta. The **silt** deposited by the

river as it slows down forms a network of channels and islands known as "the flats." It is one of the world's greatest shorebird habitats. More than 15 million birds are believed to stop there on their journeys north and south to summer and winter feeding grounds.

The cold waters of the river are the breeding grounds for pacific salmon. Brown bears, black bears, otters, wolves, and moose are all found around the delta.

 The North Slope wetlands are one of the world's remotest places. They also contain about one-third of the United States' oil reserves.

The North Slope

The North Slope coastal tundra is a vast area of boggy ground in northern Alaska. It stretches over an area of 88,000 square miles (228,800 sq km) from the mountains of the

Brooks Range to the Pacific Ocean. The North Slope is one of the world's greatest wilderness areas. Just 9,000 people live in an area that is as big as all of Great Britain. Numerous lakes form when the land thaws in the short-lived Arctic summer. Shallow rivers and streams cut across the landscape as it slopes gently from the mountains to the ocean. Caribou, bears, and musk oxen roam the tundra.

Wetlands and Waterfowl

Wetlands are an important habitat for many different kinds of birds. The muddy soils are often rich in insects, **mollusks**, and other small prey animals. Wetlands also provide many places for safe breeding and **roosting**.

Salt marshes in particular are very important as habitats for vast numbers of water birds such as ducks and geese. Because the salt marshes do not freeze as easily as the freshwater marshes, birds move there in the winter to feed. Birds that breed in the northern tundra, for example, fly south to coastal marshlands in the winter.

Freshwater swamps also have a rich variety of bird life. Herons, with their long legs and necks, move easily through the reeds hunting for fish and frogs.

Shapes and sizes

Each type of wetland bird has its own unique beak and leg length. This means that they each look for food in different depths of water and can probe into different depths of mud in their search for food. Some are able to dive and can

The heron's long neck is an adaptation to life in the wetlands.

The feathers of the bittern help it stay hidden from predators among the reeds.

therefore **forage** in deep water. Others can only duck their heads beneath the water, limiting their reach to the length of their necks. All of this variety means that the birds aren't competing with each other for food. They are all after something different.

Wetland plants give birds shelter from the wind and rain as well as from other animals. While some animals might be reluctant to go out into the water to hunt young birds, there are others, such as alligators, turtles, and varieties of big fish, that are perfectly happy to do so. Some birds blend in with the water plants around them by having feathers that look streaky. This **camouflage** helps hide birds such as the bittern and some herons from hunters. It is even more effective when the birds sit still and point their beaks upward.

What Wetlands Do

Wetlands lie between water habitats, such as rivers or seas, and dry land habitats, playing a vital role in maintaining the health of both. Among the services performed by wetlands are defense against flooding, **erosion** control, and water filtering. They also provide excellent temporary homes for migrating animals such as birds.

Flood defense

Natural flood plains, which include wetlands, are like giant, shallow bowls that soak up water and prevent flood damage to land farther away from a flooding river. Wetland plants help to slow down the flow of floodwater so it can sink into and be absorbed by the soil more easily. Like large sponges, wetlands can take up floodwater quickly and then slowly release it back to the rivers and lakes.

Erosion control

By slowing down the flow of water along rivers, and absorbing floodwater, wetlands help prevent the erosion of the surrounding land. Without wetlands, running water would wash away soil over a wide area, taking valuable nutrients with it. Wetland plants also hold soil in

 Wetlands are a valuable defense against flooding, soaking up excess water and then slowly releasing it back into area rivers and streams.

 The Congaree Swamp is just one of the countless wetlands that helps keep the world's water clean.

place with their roots. Coastal wetlands such as salt marshes act as natural barriers against potentially damaging, storm-blown waves crashing in from the sea.

Water filters

Wetlands help to improve water quality in a number of ways. They act like filters, removing chemicals from the water and trapping sediment as water passes through. The abundant populations of bacteria in the wetland mud break down organic wastes and pollutants, cleaning the water up before it returns to the rivers.

WETLAND VALUE

A study carried out in 1990 showed that the Congaree Bottomland Hardwood Swamp, in South Carolina, removes a quantity of pollutants from the water that would be the same as that handled by a $5 million wastewater treatment plant.

Wetlands also act as reservoirs. They release some of the water they collect from rainfall, rivers, and streams back into the rivers and into the water table.

Wetlands under Threat

For many people, a wetland is simply a piece of wet, muddy ground to be drained and built upon or used for **agriculture**. As the world's population increases, and pressure grows to find land for human use, wetlands are being increasingly threatened—and they are disappearing fast.

One of the main reasons for the shrinking number of wetlands is the need to find land and water to grow crops to feed a growing population. Drainage of underground water supplies for **irrigation** lowers the water table and destroys wetlands. Wetlands can easily be converted to agricultural land by draining. More than half of the wetland areas that once existed in the United States have been drained and are now used for agriculture. Some wetlands are being converted to farmland without being drained first. They are used in much the same way as the waterlogged rice paddy fields of Southeast Asia.

Although wetlands can absorb pollutants to a certain extent, agricultural chemical runoff and industrial waste pose severe threats to their health. If crop fertilizers seep into a wetland habitat, they can cause fast-growing plants to spring up alarmingly.

Rice paddies are examples of wetlands being converted for agricultural use. Native wetland plants are not allowed to grow.

▲ *Three areas of the Danube River's delta have been included in Ramsar's list of wetlands.*

The slow-growing, native wetland plants can't compete, and the nature of the habitat can be changed forever. Oil spills washing ashore can devastate a salt marsh.

What can be done?

In 1971, representatives of many of the world's nations met in Ramsar, Iran, to sign a convention, or agreement, setting out ideas for the wise use of wetlands. Today, 136 countries are members of Ramsar. Each member country has promised to do three things:

I) To manage and promote the wise use of all wetlands within their territory;

II) To consult with other members on the best ways to meet the aims of the convention, especially with regard to

wetlands that cross international borders;

III) To nominate wetlands to be included in Ramsar's List of Wetlands of International Importance for Conservation. So far, eight percent of the world's wetlands, an area larger than Portugal, have been included in Ramsar's list.

The Ramsar Convention on Wetlands has done a lot to change people's attitudes toward wetlands. Its "Working for Wetlands" program, for example, has provided funds to train and employ thousands of people in South Africa to look after the wetlands there and the supply of clean water they can provide. However, more can be done. Some countries have been slow to nominate sites for protection. Others have built over supposedly protected sites. The battle to protect the world's wetlands goes on.

Glossary

adapted Suited to life in a particular environment.

agriculture The practice of growing crops for human or animal food and of keeping domesticated (tamed) animals such as cattle and sheep.

biomes Large areas of the environment with distinctive climates and plant types; examples include forests, mountains, and deserts.

bogs Wetlands found where temperatures are low and the soil is lacking in nutrients.

buttresses Types of roots found growing from the lower part of the trunk of many tropical wetland trees; buttresses give the tree extra support in the wet soil.

camouflage The markings, shape, or coloration that an animal may have that make it difficult to see against the background.

climate The general weather conditions in a particular area.

delta The area where a river spreads out as it slows down and flows into the sea.

erosion The wearing away of the earth's surface by the action of agents such as wind, water, and temperature changes.

evaporates Changes from a liquid into a vapor (gas) without boiling; puddles of rainwater disappear as they evaporate in the sunshine.

forage Search for food.

germinate Start to grow; when a seed grows and produces its first root and leaves, it has germinated.

glaciers Slow-moving rivers of ice that move down from the snowfields at the tops of mountains.

habitat The place where a living thing makes its home; the environment that it is adapted to survive in.

irrigation Supplying water to the land by artificial means such as channels.

marsh A low-lying wetland area.

migrating Moving from one place to another in search of better living conditions.

minerals Chemicals that must be present in a healthy diet; different minerals are used in a variety of ways, including growth and the regulation of the body's activities.

mollusks A group of animals without backbones; most live in the sea, but some are found in fresh water, and a few, such as slugs and snails, live on land.

nutrients Another word for food; all the things needed for a balanced diet to provide energy and raw materials for growth and maintenance of the organism.

peat A substance formed by the incomplete breakdown of dead plant materials in bogs.

predators Animals that catch and eat other animals for food.

prey Animals that are caught and eaten by predators.

reservoirs Places where large amounts of water are stored.

roosting Settling in a resting place to sleep for the night.

sediment Loose material such as sand or soil that settles out from water and falls to the bottom.

silt A type of fine sediment usually found on river bottoms.

stands Areas where one type of tree is dominant, such as an oak stand.

tide The regular rising and falling of the sea level around the shores of the world's seas and oceans; tides are influenced by the gravity of the moon and sun.

tundra Region of the cold north where there is a layer of permanently frozen soil beneath the topsoil; few trees can grow, and the vegetation is mainly grasses and mosses.

water table The upper level of the groundwater, the water collected under the surface of the ground.

Index